Stallion's Crag
haiku prose poems of Wales

Ken Jones

IRON
PRESS

First published 2003 by IRON Press
5 Marden Tce, Cullercoats, Northumberland
England, NE30 4PD
Tel/Fax: +44 (0) 191 253 1901
Email: seaboy@freenetname.co.uk
website: www.ironpress.co.uk
ISBN 0 906228 84 0

cover and book design by IRONeye @ IRON Press
cover photo, Ken Jones

IRON Press books are distributed by Central Books
IRON Press is represented by
Inpress Ltd
1st Floor
52 Harpur St
Bedford
MK40 2QT
Tel: +44 (0)1234 330023
Fax: +44 (0) 1234 330024
Email: jon@inpressbooks.co.uk
Web: www.inpressbooks.co.uk

Ken Jones———

Ken Jones is a co-editor of the annual volume *Contemporary Haibun* . He contributes regularly to UK haiku magazines, and is represented in British and American anthologies. He has been awarded the Sasakawa Prize for Original Contributions in the Field of Haiku, and in 2002 he acted as UK judge for the first Nobuyuki Yuasa International English Haibun Contest.

For the most part the present volume presents Jones's earlier work. In 2001 he co-authored *Pilgrim Foxes*: *Haiku and Haiku Prose*, with James Norton and Sean O'Connor (Pilgrim Press, Aberystwyth). His most recent haibun appear in *Arrow of Stones* (2002), a bilingual English and Japanese publication by the British Haiku Society. Both of these volumes contain Welsh interest material.

Jones is a Zen practitioner of thirty years' standing, and author of books on socially engaged Buddhism. He lives in Ceredigion with his Irish wife, Noragh.

Contents————

Preface ──────────

The title piece, *Stallion's Crag*, is based on my experience of several years roaming Pumlumon (Plynlimon), "the sacred mountain of Wales". It is a literary creation rather than a documented record of history and fable. What it is really about is best left for the reader to decide. It is significant, however, that I have told my story as a haibun. This is an ancient Japanese literary form which blends haiku and haiku-like prose.

There has been a growing interest in haiku in the West in recent years and some consensus has emerged as to what makes a good haiku. Haiku is the expression of a momentary objective experience: simple, clear, direct. It is not an amusing little aphorism or any three line anecdote that may have occurred to the writer. It avoids subjective poetic embellishment, and the wordiness, abstraction, and philosophising that commonly go with it. Instead it prefers allusion and understatement, leaving space for the reader's own response. Thus haiku writers express their feelings through the images they use, rather than telling their readers how *sad* or *lonely* they feel. Some haiku are cameos of deeply felt imagery. Some -- called senryu -- touch on the endearing follies of human beings. Others go further, presenting unexpected and contrasting images, which can convey layers of subtle and ambiguous meaning. There may be a momentary and elusive shift in the reader's experience of reality, a mysterious whiff of something strange yet somehow familiar. This relates to the Zen Buddhist tradition in haiku which inspires my own writing { 1 }.

Both haiku and haibun were pioneered by the influential Matsuo Basho (1644-1694), and there are several English translations of his haibun masterpiece *Narrow Road to the Deep North*. In the West the haibun has developed as a poor relation of haiku, and there is not the same consensus as to what makes a quality haibun. My own concern is for a prose of strong haiku character, and with the elliptical quality, the allusiveness, ambiguity and paradox of classic haiku. When these characteristics are combined with a concern for history, myth and literary association, haibun may take on an ironic postmodern tone. { 2 }

Much of my information about Pumlumon people and places comes from Erwyd Howells of Capel Madog, Pumlumon shepherd and an authority on the folk history of north Ceredigion. I am extremely grateful to him for his helpfulness and enthusiasm. There is also an interesting published collection of reminiscences, *O Gwmpas Pumlumon*, by another local man, J.M. Davies { 3 }.

The haibun *Stallion's Crag* owes much to the example and encouragement of David Cobb, a past president of the British Haiku Society. His two long pieces *A Day in Twilight* and the earlier *Spring Journey to the Saxon Shore* are a fine demonstration of what this ancient yet novel literary form is capable { 4 }. I am grateful to David, and to my wife Noragh, for reading and commenting upon the drafts of all the material in this collection. My thanks are also due to Peter Finch, for his ready support when first faced with this novel literary animal.

Communion has appeared in the *New Welsh Review*. However, most of the material was first published in specialist haiku magazines: *Blithe Spirit*, *Haiku Spirit*, *Haiku Presence*, and *Snaphots*. The present volume owes much to the support and encouragement of the editors of these high-quality publications. Colin Blundell, the current editor of *Blithe Spirit*, has been particularly concerned to promote haibun as an authentic literary genre.

Wales has the rare distinction that two of its prominent mainstream poets, Peter Finch and Nigel Jenkins, both publish fine, authentic haiku.{ 5 } It is my hope that this collection will encourage others, on both sides of Offa's Dyke, to try their hands at haiku and haibun.

Foreword —————————

I've often stomped my way across the bogs of
Wales, through its crags, its screes, its peaks and
sheep trails, its valley heads and precipices, its
paths and outcrops, its tracks and cols, and
considered how best such an experience might
be recorded. Once the town is behind you and
you get nearer the sky there is an urge somehow
to make something of this. Others have tried --
many of them. Jim Perrin's striking prose of the
North Wales peaks, the late Alfred Wainwright's
hand-drawn guidebooks which mix track,
history and Lake District observation, and, of
course, that now ancient classic of backwoods
walking, Matsuo Basho's *Narrow Road to the Deep
North*. But, once over, the experience is so
difficult to pin down. How do to put the rain in
there? What of the history staring back at you
from the stones? And the people you've met en-
route. Where do they go?

   The Japanese haibun, a place where haiku and
taut prose meet, may well be an appropriate
vehicle. Alien in Wales, land of *englynion*, but
somehow appropriate. We may not have plum

blossom on the slopes, but the feeling you get as you hack across them can be much the same. Ken Jones has spent a lot of his life crossing Pumlumon and trying to dissolve what he experiences into haiku. In *Stallion's Crag*, a splendid mix of poetry and prose, he has drawn together much of what he has found and made art from it. Not quite history, not just travelogue, not simply observation of the echoes we make as we band up against nature but all three in controlled mix -- "a mysterious whiff of something strange yet somehow familiar". Read it slowly. Imagine Pumlumon's wetness and then its sun emerging. Harri Webb called this place the green desert. It's absolutely that.

Peter Finch

Peter Finch is a poet and short story writer. He runs the Academi, the Welsh national literature promotion agency and society of writers.

Stallion's Crag

The black tarmac strip comes to an end.
The motor disappears back into the
mountain silence. Down by the stream is a
reception committee.

> *Three crows in a bare tree*
> *proclaim the meaning of life*
> *as usual*

I give them a wave.
Ahead lies a broad valley. Great hills rise
on every side, the grey bones of the
mountain showing through their flanks.
Here and there fans of scree spill down the
slopes, and boulders litter the brown bogs.
This is now a vast sheep walk, roadless,
ruined and depopulated -- a tumbled world
of mist and bog, of looming and elusive
shapes. There was once a notice at the
farmhouse of Eisteddfa Gurig announcing
that "The Notorious Hill of Plinlimmon is
on the Premises and will be shown to any
Gentleman Travellers who wish to see it."

All the literati who took up the offer seem
to have had a bad time; Thomas Love
Peacock, for example, wrote in 1855 about
getting lost and soaked to the skin. And all
this despite repeated warnings from the
guidebook writers. One declared that "The
Voluptuary will find little in this region to
detain him." And Benjamin Malkin, in 1804,
warned that "it affords little food for the
picturesque enthusiasms of those who
venture on the laborious perils of the
ascent". He added that "it is the most
dangerous mountain in Wales ... and should
not be attempted without a guide, whose
attendance is very precarious."

I soon dismissed this bleak, featureless
wasteland when I first came here as a youth
in search of excitement. Even today there is
only one car park, unofficial and usually
empty. Instant drama begins further north,
on Cadair Idris. There, if you spend only a
night on the summit you will at least
awaken either mad or a poet. Pumlumon
takes longer. Half a century in my case.

Back on the mountain
my grey beard
soaking up the mist

Here at the road's end there's a keen wind blowing. Cold and rain are kept out by closely woven cotton, over finely spun lambswool, over Welsh flannel, over Japanese silk, over mortal skin. Dyed field grey, head to foot, and lightly waxed. Buckled snug down to the hips is a well worn backpack, with five days of green tea, frankincense, midge repellent, and much else, but not a word to read.

Contentedness
of mist and bog
miles of trudging solitude

It is said that once upon a time a squirrel could leap from tree to tree the whole sixteen miles between Llanidloes and Machynlleth church towers. This thickly wooded wilderness was home to a glorious company of saints and outlaws, poets and

patriots, shepherds and hymnographers.
Here the forgotten dead mingle with the
mythically alive. Cairns were built on the
summits to propitiate the demons of place,
to avoid getting lost and, later on, to
commemorate local weddings. Today in this
bare landscape only place names bear
witness, like Nant Gelligogau:

> *Cuckoo Grove Dell*
> *a peaty cut*
> *forgotten on a treeless moor*

Finally, the central valley itself, Nant y
Moch, below where I stand, was flooded in
1964 to drive electric turbines. During the
great 1904 revival fervent congregations of
fifty or more had raised the *hwyl* in the tiny
Methodist chapel.

> *From broken farms*
> *to the drowned chapel*
> *busy footpaths dip beneath the waves*

In 1960 the two ancient James brothers who
remained were displaced from their

whitewashed farmhouse next to the chapel.
And the following year the dead were dug
up too and reburied in *terra firma*. John
James had looked after the sheep and cattle,
and his brother the chickens and their
excellent theological library. At the time
they were moved one was over 80 and the
other twelve years younger. Both had long
passages of scripture by heart, and had
turned many a fine *englyn* and *cywydd* in
their time. { 6 } This was a breed of God-
driven folk, hotly arguing about theological
niceties as they worked at the peats high on
the *mynydd* in the thin westerly rains. After
the flood the brothers were offered a
breeze-block bungalow built for them at the
road's end. Now on the ruined barn,
corrugated iron clangs and rattles.

> *Bitter wind*
> *warm tears*
> *dry in an instant*

The last gate in more than a dozen miles
closes behind me. Across the valley I catch

sight of a few tumbled stones, marked by
three ash trees in an old rick yard
overgrown with nettles. They left in 1952.
I wish I knew their name.

   Close by my track lies a few yards of
drystone walling. It goes nowhere, but the
workmanship is skilful. They say it was
built long ago on the morning of a wedding
by the groom and his best man. Shelters
sheep in bad weather. This track goes on
and on...

   Crunch of boots
   hands behind my back
                      trailing
                         mind

   Winding down now to the ruins of Nant y
Llyn, once the biggest farm hereabouts. In
1919, after the Great War, the old people
sold up and left. Now trees taller than a
man grow in parlour and kitchen, protected
from the nibbling sheep.

Faint paths
tumbled walls
silence of mist

However, on a sun-bright day there is a liveliness here. The track crosses the infant Rheidol with a skip and jump and then swings left to a more serious ford through the Hengwm. The labyrinth of ruined stone pens shows that this was once a gathering place for livestock. Great rotting posts stand here and there, now left to themselves.

Tautness of rusty wire --
feeling the pull
of a dead man

II

Of all the ghosts who haunt these hills by far the most illustrious is Owain Glyndwr, Prince of Wales -- statesman and shaman, soldier and mystic, and perennial national hero. The profane can now dine off commemorative six hundredth anniversary plates from the National Library. It was at Hyddgen, near here, that Glyndwr's half-starved liberation army won its first victory in the war of independence. In the summer of 1401 a punitive expedition of English and Flemings marched into the mountain. They were doubtless spurred on by a rumour put about by King Henry's agents that if Glyndwr were victorious the English would all be forced to learn Welsh ! Owain's band amounted to a mere "120 reckless men and robbers". { 7 } Thomas Ellis, the eighteenth century antiquarian, adds a bit of wordy drama:

Finding themselves surrounded and hard put to it, [the Welsh] resolved to make their way through or perish in the attempt: so falling on furiously with courage whetted by despair, they put the enemy, after sharp dispute, to confusion; they pursued so eagerly their advantage, that they made them give ground, and in the end to fly outright, leaving two hundred of their men dead on the spot of engagement. { 8 }

It was little more than an out-of-the-way skirmish, and yet there is something about the place. R. S. Thomas wrote a poem

about it. And *Deffro* (*Awakening*) is the title
of another, by Iorwerth Jones, Aberhosan,
which won him a chair at the 1977 Powys
Eisteddfod. Early one morning, on Carn
Hyddgen above the site of the battle, he
had a compelling vision. "The poetry
overwhelmed me. It was hours before I
could get home and write it -- 160 lines."

Near the battle site is a well-watered fold
in the hills -- Siambr Trawsfynedd, which
some believe was Glyndwr's base. Years
ago, hastening home in twilight through
that wild place, I was surprised to see two
figures ahead. One radiated a regal
presence even at that distance. The other
looked to be in clerical garb. Was it
Glyndwr's faithful secretary, Rhisiart?
Strolling, conferring, gesturing, they
disappeared behind a crag. Some local
shepherds refer to "the Prince" as if he were
still a local resident. Perhaps he is. "Myn
Duw, mi wn y daw" ("My God, I know he
will come") sings the national pop star
Dafydd Iwan:

Our hero still --
striding the moonlit ford
in antique leathers

Across the river from Nant y Llyn are two
white quartz boulders, the Cerrig Cyfamod
Glyndwr -- Stones of the Covenant. One
legend has it that here Earl Edmund
Mortimer made a compact with the Prince,
who had taken him hostage. Edmund is an
interesting and tragic figure. He married
Glyndwr's daughter and perished of
starvation or disease in the terrible winter
siege of Harlech castle in 1408. His wife
died a prisoner in the Tower of London not
long afterwards..

Stones of the Covenant
in bog and rushes
a gleaming silence

My own way lies onwards west up the
main valley. A faint track, rutted and
waterlogged, keeps close to the river, then

loses itself in one of Pumlumon's most impressive bogs. I pick my way over dark stones -- the Graves of the Warriors, though who they were and what they might have died for, who can tell? Ahead rises a huddle of huge rocks, which together enclose several low-roofed chambers. This is Encil Craig Brwynen, my Hermitage of the Rushes.

> *Staining the roof*
> *above my coffin bed*
> *blood red lichens*

Upholstered with rushes it is nonetheless a dry and cosy coffin, though wriggling in and out of it can be a bone-chafing business. From a smaller chamber I draw out an image of Kwan Yin, the Goddess of Compassion, together with candles and incense. She has long since forgotten her early life in a Chinese grocery, and sits at ease on her ceramic lotus leaf.

Suddenly a glimpse of bright synthetics: a dozen outward bound youth in single file. Of the few people I see even in this main valley, most are too busy going somewhere to be really here. The sun glints on the leader's plastic map case. Only the last and youngest lags behind and stares about him curiously.

> *Graves of the Warriors*
> *click-clack of trekking poles*
> *young men marching*

Even here, so many different floating worlds, all caught in the goddess Indra's net of time and space.{ 9 } George Parry, Esq. disputed a boundary running through my rushes ("Marked A to B") with the Pryses of Gogerddan. Their artistic estate map of 1788 contrasts with his disputatious scrawl (though with a memo to reward a faithful shepherd scribbled in a corner).

Half a century ago the youths would have marched past a trim homestead and through fields of rippling rye. This was Hengwm Annedd, home to several generations of Morgans. Today I thread my way through clumps of reeds across poor pasture.

> *Rattling in the wind*
> *dry thistles*
> *their drifting seed*

From the kitchen door a plank bridge led straight across the river to their neighbours. It is told that one day an elderly Morgan was returning with a gift of uncommonly fine soda water, when he was taken with a seizure on the very middle of the bridge. As to the recording of his death, the poor fellow fell into an adminstrative limbo, from which neither Cardiganshire County on the one bank, nor Montgomeryshire on the other, was willing to redeem him.

The Morgans gave up their tenancy and left in 1935, and at the same time ownership of the land passed to a family called Micah. They never lived in the house, which fell into neglect. In the ruins

is a large iron bedstead which has fallen
through the vanished ceiling into the rubble
of the parlour below --

> *Matrimonial bed*
> *rusty and twisted*
> *castors spinning still*

Rummaging about I find under a pig mash
boiler a lady's slender boot, mildewed,
among shards of willow pattern. Gathered
of an evening around the family bible, did
the wearer ever ponder the prophet's
thunderous warnings to transgressors?

Therefore I will make Samaria as an heap of
the field...and I will pour down the stones
thereof into the valley, and I will discover
the foundations thereof (Micah, 1, 6).

III

Sobered, I hump my pack, find my stick,
and plod off over boulders up into a side
valley. Ahead rise the fine cliffs of Yr
Eglwys -- The Steeple. In a blue sky waves

of mist break and dissolve around rock
pinnacles. The Afon Gwerin is in spate,
foaming through its smooth rock channel.
Flinging my pack across into a reed bed, I
take a running jump.

> *Between two slippery rocks*
> *mid   air*
> ***only this !***

Like much else here The Steeple is not what
it appears to be. Its backside stretches away
into desolate moorland, distinguished only
by a large sparkling lump of quartz close to
a smaller one -- Fuwch-wen-a'r-llo, the Cow
& Calf. Tucked away in a little nant is Y
Fagwr, the drystone house. Even for
Pumlumon this is a lonely and forlorn ruin:
tumbled lichened stones among bog and
rushes, with a few stonechats doing their
best. A family called Humfreys lived here,
probably until the end of the nineteenth
century. Their departure may have been
hastened by a strange occurrence. One day
the woman of the house went to visit a

distant farm. She never came back. Only her shopping basket was ever found, lying empty.

My way, however, lies west up the wild valley of the Gwerin. Its entrance is guarded by a crag, surmounted by the only pine in a dozen miles. Dramatically bonsai'd by the westerlies, it has survived the sheep by growing out of a deep cleft. On my first visit I lost my compass down that hole, and slid down the tree after it, into the dark acrid smell of fox.

> *Fox spirit's den*
> *cold against my shin*
> *white bone*

A shepherd once told me that the Ordnance Survey's "Gwerin" is a missprint for "Gwarin" --a fox warren. Fox -- trickster and shape-shifter of the animal kingdom; Cwm Gwarin is a foxy place. In all my years here I have only met people on two occasions, the first being a pair of hunters. They ranged the head of the valley with gun and dogs but it gave them no sport. The second were a young couple, seriously lost.

As to that solitary pine, my hermit name is *Coeden ar yr Mynydd* ("Tree on the Mountainside"), -- *I Ching* hexagram 53. There is a wonderful word *disgwylfa*, for a place of watching and watchfulness. On a sunny afternoon I ramble down from my base at the head of the cwm, offer incense at Encil Brwynen, chant blessings for the shades of Hengwm Annedd, and sit under the pine here at Disgwylfa Coeden ar yr Mynydd. These vigils are shared by a mythic senior member of the profession. Somewhere on a bracken-infested belvedere, higher up among the cliffs, lies Ffynnon Esgob -- Bishop's Spring. But I have never found it.

> *No Holy Well --*
> *stone saucer of rain*
> *ripples in the wind*

Time to get on, now crossing a broad vein

of quartz. In the early lean time of the year
fleeces of dead lambs lie among the white
boulders, with the blackness of crows
hopping from one to the other.

> *Slim pelvis*
> *slender legs*
> *sheep skeleton*

Swinging back towards the river I pass a
pool beneath a slippery outcrop. Once
upon a time Ifan lent his horse to Siôn, and
it was just Siôn's bad luck that it was his
neighbour's animal that lost its footing here
and drowned. If it's going to happen, it'll
happen to something borrowed from a
neighbour. Yes, Sod's Law, or, up here,
"Pwll Siôn, ceffyl Ifan" -- "John's pool,
Evan's horse". But it also says something
else, about the high value placed on trust
by people who so much depended on each
other.

This bare landscape was once alive with
names, many signalling myths and stories --

even history and biography. They mapped a landscape of collective memory. It is a land now largely denuded of meaning as well as of trees, but unlike the trees, what has been lost can no more be replaced -- ever -- than can the species of plants and creatures that disappear each year in this great die-off. A few disembodied fragments are mercifully retained on the large scale Ordnance Survey maps. For instance, the map shows on the opposite side of the cwm from here a "Lluest y Graig" ("Crag Farm"), but no amount of poking about has revealed the remains of any building nor can anyone remember one.

Weighed down by these melancholy reflections I blunder through the Afon Felen, heedless of what a lively, gracious little character it is, with its mossy falls.

> *Sliding softly*
> *over green baize*
> *the Yellow River*

Half way up the cwm is a riverside place of

rest and refreshment. And if its standing
stone is not a *Standing Stone* then it should
be. Such an erection sustained for three
millennia deserves respect.

> *Phallic stone*
> *its ginger lichens*
> *lambswool*
> *blowing in the wind*

Propping myself against the sunny side, I
ease off my boots, cut a wedge of *bara brith,*
top it with black-rind goat's cheese, get the
spirit stove going for coffee at the first try,
enjoy my company, and count my blessings.
Loitering with intent.

> *Through dimpled water*
> *yellow pebbles*
> *washed in yellow light*

I recall walking here with Erwyd, a
shepherd friend. *Llonc a clonc,* saunter and
chat -- the only way I can keep up with
him. A bottle of Lucozade sticks out of one

pocket and a wire brush out of the other, for scraping off moss and lichens. We are looking for names and dates cut in the rocks by shepherds long ago. To meet anyone here would be remarkable, but the distant figure across the valley is even more remarkable. I put the glass on him. The pied synthetics of your state-of-the-art walker. A strange looking dog too.

> *Big country --*
> *to greet a far-off stranger*
> *a whole arm*

But this sets the stranger scuttling off as if he were hurrying to catch the 8.23 from Tunbridge Wells or some similarly outlandish place. *Sais?*, mutters Erwyd, then bellows a greeting in the language of heaven: *Sut ydych chi heddiw?* At this the stranger starts as if he had been shot, makes a curious gesture, and changes course up the side of the cwm. Puzzled, we gaze at his departing back, our two pairs of boots settling gently in the bog.

Here now are the first hermetic works:
little cairns marking a way through livid
green bog to Craig y March.

> *Lapped by bracken*
> *looming through red mist*
> *high prow of Stallion's Crag*

IV

A grassy rake angles breathlessly upwards.
Then there's the heart-thumping steepness
of a stony shelf. This in turn becomes
narrow and airy. At nightfall, descending
with a handful of dirty dishes, a foolish
place to be.

My cave is no more than an overhang in
the cliff, with a fern-hung rockfall to keep
out the wind. The interior is bright with
lichens and pungent with sheep shit. Maybe
St Curig, the Irish missionary, was the first
distinguished resident, staring out through
the same mist fourteen centuries ago. Did

the mountain she-devil invade his dreams?

> *Her heaving flanks*
> *her flashing falls*
> *love song in the wind*

Glyndwr must surely have passed some nights here, for he dossed in more Welsh caves than Queen Elizabeth slept in English beds. Another resident could well have been the great fifteenth century bard Lewys Glyn Cothi. On the wrong side at the battle of Mortimer's Cross in 1461, he became a Pumlumon outlaw. In happier times "he sang much to the gentry of Carmathenshire, Cardiganshire and Radnorshire," working their coats of arms in colour into his manuscripts. On a nearby rock face a more recent visitor has chiselled his name: **John J Morgan, Tach** [November] **1928**. This could have been one John Jenkin Morgan, Hengwm Annedd, drowned of a cramp after haymaking, only a few months later.

Creeping up the mountain
consuming the day
the shadow

There is much to do. A stone rolled aside reveals a cache of stores: candles and canned lentils; a tin opener and latrine scoop. The sheep dung is swept out, rushes cut to make a bed, and a drystone wind break heaped up. With billy can and water bottle I climb above the crag to a tiny grotto. The little Buddha, his hand in blessing, is slowly turning green in the plashing spring. Back to the cave, and sizzling vegetarian Carmarthen sausages. The couple in the flat above, a pair of elderly ravens, are already quarrelling, scattering twigs and turds down the cliff face. After dark I have an occasional neighbour, a big mysterious snuffler on the other side of the rock fall. We have always respected one another's privacy.

Yet another visit, yet another latrine dug in the same peaty patch:

> *Marking my dead latrines*
> *one after another*
> *little tombstones*

From thence there's a scramble over a reef
of rock and down steep grass to the
washing place by the river. If the timing's
right, the midges will have gone to bed.
The toothpaste cap is perched always on
the same big lump of Ordovician slate. It is
handsomely decorated by extruded bands
of white quartz, beside which my
toothpaste is also carefully extruded. This is
a good time and place to lose Small Objects:

> *In the pebbles of the stream*
> *my delicate pink dental plate*

Chores completed, sitting on a rock, the
busyness subsides, and the mountain
breathes again.

Before turning in I take a meditative turn
on the flat top of the crag.

> *Seventy years --*
> *in that gun-metal tarn*
> *another dying day*

Also still visible through the gloaming are those two big mysterious cairns. I muse about the shadowy Gwilym after whom they may be named. The stallion of Stallion's Crag is Grey Fetlocks (Llwyd y Bacsiau), Glyndwr's great war horse. Galloping across the crag in one death-defying leap he delivered the hero from his pursuers.

> *In the falling light*
> *soft rain*
> *in rock hoof prints*

I grope my way down back to the cave, the flickering candle lantern a small delight. My sleeping bag is already stretched out peacefully.

What kind of night will it be? Sometimes the clouds clear from the mountain and I am moon-struck. Wide awake, I listen to my most constant companions:

In floods of moonlight
enchanted stonechats
sing the night away

Pulling on my boots and tip-toeing down
the crag, I wander off in the soft cheesy
light, taking my strange nocturnal shadow
with me. And, just once, aghast at a
familiar strangeness:

Bathed in moonlight
Sister Anima
my full-breasted self

But mostly Pumlumon is soaked in every
kind of *wetness*, for days and even weeks
on end. It was an all night storm some
years ago that ended my romantic
honeymoon with the mountain -- all those
exquisite poems and brush drawings
celebrating the life of Ch'an and Taoist
hermits and nature-loving Celtic saints.
Forked lightning flashed along Tor Glas,
the ridge opposite. Thunder shook the
mountain and cannonaded round the cwm.
Rain curtained off the front of my cave,

pouring down the cliff face above. And
within, every nook and cranny sprung a
leak. Came the dawn -

> *Damp goose down bag*
> *a svelte brown slug*
> *creeps in beside me*

Sometimes a starless night of damp stillness
hangs over the mountain, amplifying
whatever sounds there are.

> *Somewhere in the mist*
> *a sheep's hacking cough*
> *the night wears on*

The dawn landscape is narrowed to the
reeds which fringe the front of the cave,
each delicately beaded with drops of water.
As the stove struggles to produce the first
coffee of the day, on some mornings a
miracle occurs. The sun cranks up behind
the ridge opposite, pouring blinding light
and instant warmth straight into the cave.
Leaning back I gaze across to where the

Princes of Arwystli lie waiting to be called.

> *Slanting rays*
> *thinning the white mists*
> *that drift across the princes' graves*

V

"How interesting, but what do hermits actually *do*?" she asked, balancing a wine glass in one hand.

The main concern of this one is not to be in the same place and time as the clouds of midges which share my habitat:

> This midge
> **like me**
> enjoys the hazy sunshine

In fact this hermit's job description is a blank; just bare attention, *disgwylgar*, to be all here and not somewhere else, and to let the mountain do the rest. Mind is free to wander as it will in the first day or two, but never far. Gradually it homes in to the steep slopes of so many shades of brown and green, grey screes and cliffs, mists creeping along the ridges, the bark of ravens, the call of sheep, the little stonechats. Sometimes attention is drawn fifteen inches away:

> *This old rock lump*
> *mosses and lichens*
> *every inch*

Sometimes it's fifteen miles away;

> *Cadair Idris*
> *lion couchant*
> *floating on a cloud*

Huge blocks of empty time confront me. When the weather closes in and confines me, time stretches out, emptiness deepens. All there is is too much wetness, too much mist, too much battering wind, too many maddening midges. The words of the Zen sage Seng Ts'an come to mind:

Cease from action, and rest itself becomes restless;
linger over either extreme and Oneness is forever
lost. { 10 }

 In the cave there is only room to crouch, so
I sit nearby in a tolerably dry cleft. When I
get cold, stiff and damp, I pace up and
down the ledge in front of me. I watch the
rain fall. I watch the curtain of mist, which
sometimes lifts a little to reveal a bit of
mountain. There is nothing else to watch
except my own frustration, which soon
becomes as boring as everything else. All
those "B" movies projected in the skull
cinema, whether trailers or vintage
screenings. Already all too familiar. All
escape routes cut off, I'm now my own
inescapable problem. Driven silly enough,
it becomes easier to just let it be. So, sooner
or later the monkey gives up, and the
mountain claims its own. Glyndwr's leap to
freedom! Except that he just clung on and
Grey Fetlocks carried him ... which is how
it happens.

> *Sheep shit and incense*
> *sunshine and drizzle*
> *the unchanging view*

So, at seventeen hundred feet, I practice the Zen of Just-Hanging-Out, with different rocks and perches to mark the changing shifts of sun, wind and rain.

The cave and its rocky *disgwylfa* have a strong masculine feel -- dry, bright and hard, with that home-made standing stone to drive home the message. The meditation rock -- Y Castell -- where I sit time out of mind and mind out of time, commands a panoramic view.

> *Mountain wind*
> *through my ribcage*
> *already*

If there's sun, I follow it down from the yang to the yin of the Blaen Gwerin, where the valley head stream manifests the goddess. Skirts of underwater moss flare in

the pools, beneath the smart green facings
of the waterfalls. The *blaen* is a place of soft-
flowing ease, like up on that heather-clad
basking rock,

> *Snapping off*
> *black heather twigs --*
> *the whiteness!*

And downstream is the laundry rock,
another beguiling spot.

> *The current*
> *snatching away my shirt --*
> *those two blue butterflies!*

Higher up the valleyhead from a rock
oratory Kwan Yin contemplates the little
streams rushing down from their gathering
grounds

> *Swirling china robe*
> *her enigmatic smile*
> *heart of the mountain*

Over the years I have become more aware

of the power of such places. As if impelled by some magnetic field, I have been moved to amplify these channels and knots of energy with well placed cairns and stones.

VI

On a sunny afternoon there may even be an *excursion* planned: a little flutter of anticipation in the landscape of mind.

In one direction, along a broad windswept ridge, are two posts in a bog -- a God-forsaken spot even on Pumlumon. They make nowhere somewhere. For these are the insecure bilingual markers of the *true* source of the Hafren or, if you prefer, the Severn. Stones are hard to come by hereabouts. Sometimes I find them piled up around an upright Welsh "**Hafren**", leaving a sagging English "**Severn**", and sometimes they have been shifted the other way round. But never half-and-half. It is a drear and toilsome plod up from the car, following a line of linguistically blank guideposts. Finally arriving at such a place, featureless apart from "the language issue", what else to do but make a point, by shifting -- or not shifting -- a few stones? George Borrow, that garrulous Victorian traveller through "Wild Wales", also found this to be "rather a shabby source for so noble a stream". However, "it is not only necessary for me to see the sources of the rivers, but to drink them, in order that in after times I might be able to harangue about them with a tone of confidence and authority."

The source lies in a labyrinth of "unsightly heaps of black turf-earth", as Borrow called these looming peat hags, some slimy and some dried up, some shapeless and some sculpted by nature to resemble hags. Never a dull moment on this dull mountain. They cry out for silly verses:

> *In the vast bog*
> *this hag fenced in*
> *why her? Why?!*

> *Prussian blue tarn*
> *surrounded*
> *by elegant hags*

> *Not to be passed*
> *with uncaring glance*
> *this bog hole has* **attitude** *!*

In the opposite direction is the excursion to Pen Pumlumon Fawr, the highest of the five summits. The start is a stiff pull up behind Stallion's Crag, meeting with more variations on the theme of slate and quartz:

> *In hanging mist*
> *a charnel ground*
> *grey rocks flecked white*

Above, the almost featureless ridge is a great place to savour Pumlumon mist. It can even turn a cryptic metaphor for the spiritual search:

> *Alone in the mist*
> *still trying*
> *to get lost*

Ahead lies the most desolate stretch of the old upland track from Machynlleth to Llanidloes, marked at irregular intervals by fallen cairns. Here, many years ago, an old pedlar woman collapsed and died in a snow storm. As well as being a packwoman she was a welcome and well-loved visitor to the isolated homesteads, a healer, story teller and bearer of news. A stone shaped like a stooped figure marks the spot where Siân Groca -- Jane Crookback -- was found. Sad, also, to learn later that it was in fact the curious shape of the stone that inspired the story. Here the snow always lingers on.

I pick up a shard of slate to carry to the already untidy summit cairn. The ancient practice of adding your bit helped to maintain these landmarks. And if that were not reason enough then failure to do so would attract the ire of the mountain spirits and bring bad luck. This, the highest cairn, stands at 2468 feet.

In a shaft of sunlight
tiny house
never seen before

Was it seen by the Mabinogi Kai and
Bedwyr (later gentrified as Sir Kay and Sir
Bedevere), sitting up here "in the highest
wind that ever was in the world". But
certainly "they looked around them and
saw a great smoke to the south, afar off,
which did not bend in the wind." And there
began another adventure... { 11}

For the great Zen Master Dogen, sage of
mountains and rivers,

In the stream rushing past to the dusty world
my fleeting form casts no reflection { 12 }

Time now to return to that dusty world.

Of the three rivers that are Pumlimon's
daughters, Hafren and Gwy (Wye) rose
early for their long easterly journey to the
sea. Their feckless young sister, Rheidolyn,

slept in too late to be able to follow them.
So, she simply swept off west. Beautiful
throughout, day and night she ripples her
pebbles past my window. Now I keep
company with her off the mountain, down
towards the western sea.

Crimson waters
sweeping homewards
this body of joy

Notes and references

1 Ken Jones, "Zen and the art of haiku", *Blithe Spirit: Journal of the British Haiku Society,* 8(4) December 1998, 34-43.

2 On writing haibun see the Introduction to my *Arrow of Stones*, Equinox Press, Shalford (Essex), 2002.

3 J. M. Davies, *O Gwmpas Pumlumon*, Cymdeithas Llyfrau Ceredigion, Aberystwyth, 1966.

4 David Cobb, "A Day in Twilight" in *Palm*, Equinox Press, Shalford (Essex), 2002, *and Spring Journey to the Saxon Shore*, Equinox Press, Shalford, (Essex), 1997.

5. Peter Finch, *Food*, Seren, Bridgend, 2001; Nigel Jenkins, *Blue*, Planet, Aberystwyth, 2002.

6 From the *Welsh Gazette*, 16 September

1954. *Englyn*: an ancient metrical form still alive and well; its affinity with haiku is more apparent than real. *Cywydd*: another verse form, consisting of a rhyming couplet of seven syllables written in *cynghanedd*, an intricate system of sound-chiming.

7 Gruffydd Hiraethog, *Annals of Owain Glyndwr* (Peniarth MS. 135), translated in Sir John Lloyd, *History of Wales*, Longman, London, 1911.

8 Thomas Ellis, "Memoirs of Owen Glendower", being a supplement to his *History of the Island of Anglesey*, London, 1775 and subsequent editions.

9 Indra's Net: Buddhist metaphor to prompt insight into this elusive mountain. The Net is three dimensional (with time as a fourth). Each jewel (or "event") at each intersection of the Net both exists in its own right and yet also exists only as a reflection of all the other jewels. So this is an interbeing which paradoxically

transcends mere interdependence.

10 *Hsin-hsin-ming* [On trust in the Heart], probably the most widely translated of Ch'an (Zen) scriptures.

11 From "Culhwch and Olwen", in Lady Charlotte Guest's translation of the *Mabinogion*.

12 Steven Heine, *Zen Poetry of Dogen*, Tuttle Publishing, Boston, 1997. 62-J, p118.

Sheep & Conifers & Crows
and Old Grey Stones:

Mid-Wales Haiku

Solitude

On the faded carpet
window panes
printed in moonlight

Bright morning
scraping a new blade
over my bony cheek

Waiting to be helped
out of the bath
the usual spiders

After weeks of rain
surprised
by my shadow

Well-thumbed public map
You are here
no longer there

        Digging the ditch
        behind me
        a curve of new year light

Returning home
quietly
self returns to self

        On the telephone wire
        through the mist
        silent birds

Life alone
evening stillness
thickens into night

Incense burnt out
in candle light
the pink azalea

Slates
small, rough, uneven
raked by the moon

Neighbours

Dawn moon
through bare trees
light at a distant window

That kind of day
everybody's wood smoke
hangs in the air

Pale light on the Chapel Field
good morning, says Dai,
to gas the moles

First day of Spring
from wood to wood
neighbours' chainsaws chatter

"Strictly Private"
above the gate
a cloud of flies

In pale sunshine
waving   across
our disputed boundary

Strolling for miles
arm in my pocket
hoping she' ll take it

Raking out
dead neighbour's mouldy hay
o burn Guy Fawkes

Rolling home
with his stumpy shadow
and half a moon

To you, telephone pole
No. A 97381
I tip my hat

Ancient man long dead
in the rubble Plaisirs de Paris
the scent still strong

"WYAU AR WERTH"
hidden in weeds:-
"Eggs for Sale"

"Nobody about"
says the stride of the hunter
entering my yard

Through the mist
this ancient way
joining two ruins

Up by the wood
the bend in the lane
always empty

The Land

*Pushing my reflection
this wheelbarrow
full of rain*

*Condemned lambs
a bold one
holds my gaze*

*Gilded
delicately fretted
and wafer thin
this sun-dried cow pat*

*Still
as the frozen pond
the plastic duck*

*Rodding the drain
brass and bamboo
the gurgle of relief*

Old ant hills, tumbled stones
this pasture of the ancient dead
my lunch stop

Polished hooves
reflecting the sun
skeleton sheep

Evening mist
drifting along the narrow gauge
two lines of sheep

In the iron wheelbarrow
I burn leaves, push smoke
this year's vast space

Woodland

Woods
made silent
by a raven's croak

Too much grief
quietly I oil and sharpen
the old chainsaw

On my seventieth birthday
marking oaks
to be felled

In moonlight
this row of bleached stumps
my destination

Right of Way
striding into autumn bracken
a rusty little man

Dumped in a forest
the vacant stare
of a three-piece suite

Skinny birches
sky high leaves
the last to go

Walking all day
through sitka spruce
each one
different

Rusty narrow gauge
curving silently
through winter woods

This fine evening
stacking firewood
how simple death seems

Up on the Mynydd

These hills
have nothing to say
and go on saying it

> *Guiding the way*
> *heaped stones*
> *of the dead*

Birthday walk
empty landscape
mainly sky

> *Sunlight on yellow grasses*
> *on the map*
> *empty space for miles*

Europe's largest wind farm
sometimes there
sometimes not

Looking for Ireland
thirty years
nothing but sea

Mountain of false summits
even the true one
its blank stare

Sunny days --
cragfast sheep
how quietly it dies

Bronze Age
standing stone
flecked with bird shit

In the snow her boot prints
perfect
mile after mile

National Park
not a tree
out of place

> *The last of the day*
> *filling a tiny tarn*

From the mist filled cwm
the huntsman's horn
and the owl's call

> *No moon*
> *to guide me off the mountain*
> *only the flaring comet trail*

Great silent valley
year after year
for what are you waiting ?

Shorter Haibun

Red Duck Lake (Llyn Coch-Hwyad)

The Ordnance Survey's forest green is everywhere. The lake lies up high, where a skein of orange contours pulls the landscape boldly into shape.

> *Following the pecked red lines*
> *my dirty finger*
> *on the rights of way*

I struggle across a water-logged moor of yellow tussocks. Ahead lie five thousand acres of blanket conifer, the edges frayed by gales. Beyond the stile, under the dark canopy of spruce, the wind is hushed; there is only the rustle of some tiny bird. Between the rows patches of light fall on mosses and lichens. Quickening my pace along a straight dirt track I reach a forest road.

Rainbow colours of diesel oil gleam in the puddles. Bending over a pile of sticky logs I breathe deeply. Ah!

> *Pine perfume*
> *with a dash of diesel --*
> *the resin road!*

And the loggers, what austere and elegant
fellows they must be !

> *On the blackened stump*
> *a china cup*
> *of rainwater*

Tipsy on resin, I meander off along a track
beneath the candelabra of corsican pines.
And here is the cross-roads which the map
says is here. There is nothing more lonely
than a lonely cross roads. I stand in the
middle and pull my hood over my head

> *At the meeting*
> *of the five ways*
> *drifting sleet*

But the map shows only three. Which is it
to be? The compass needle kicks round,
flickers and steadies. For reassurance I

boldly point my arm, and stride off that way.

The track dwindles to a path. The path dwindles to nothing. Through a chaos of wind thrown pines is a little clearing, with a stump on which to sit lost. On the map I am nowhere in a blank green bit with only a dead midge, folded in last summer, for company.

> *Western hemlock*
> *soughing in the wind*
> *coffee's bitter taste*

Some threshing about reveals a ruckle of stones -- once a *hafody* or summer shieling on the bare upland. Beyond is the rotten stub of a fence post, and then another. After half an hour snapping branches I break out into the silence of a forest road. Each end disappears round a bend. But on the other side, under murky sitka spruce, a track rears up the bank.

Here is the first boot print of the day --
distinctive, too, a Brasher just like mine...
Who knows, in a long day's twists and
turns? But now, at last, trees thin out
against the sky.

> *Dismasted pines*
> *their riven branches*
> *point in all directions*

Below the ridge Red Duck Lake mirrors a
duck egg blue sky. A flock of snipe rises
drumming from the reeds. On the far side,
yellow rolling hills stretch to Pumlumon,
capped with snow. And below me --

> *On the still lake*
> *a sunken boat*
> *drifts among clouds*

Luxury Spring Break

"Double room in sage and apricot. It has an interesting oriel window made from an old Indian four poster bed. Dog allowed."

> *In the immaculate bath*
> *a well-groomed spider*

We exclaim at the *bonnet de douche* and the tiny phials of shampoo and "body lotion". Perhaps fellow guests are also seduced by the *appareil de bain*, because the little mountain torrent suddenly refuses to provide instant baths for all. Y Mynydd Mawr (Big Mountain) has no time for your Anglo-Norman fripperies. The "complimentary bath robe" (in salmon pink) prompts us to check the dining room dress code. "Smart casual" says the brochure, from its beaten leather cover.

In the discreet Victorian dining room heraldic escutcheons and *objets de vertu* flicker in candlelight. Ordered in Welsh, our servitors unbend.

> *Red headed waitress*
> *serves the lamb --- then*
> *back to the lambing*

The glazed monkfish pronounces itself
excellent... Gilded mirrors, heavy drapes,
high art on elevated themes adorn the
lounge. Overawed by unrelenting good
taste we sink into the armchairs and sofas.

> *Decaffeinated conversation*
> *the clink*
> *of fine boned china*

The "Full Welsh Breakfast" turns out to be
a restrained English one.

> *Taylor's English Breakfast Tea*
> *silence*
> *of couples*

The menu, however, does prove to be
intellectually challenging: orange

grapefruit, undyed Loch Fyne kippers,
coddled eggs, and black pudding, with
American muffins, Greek yoghurt and
home made marmalade to follow. Not an
eye blinks. I round off a splendid weekend
with something truly feudal.

> *Across my scrambled eggs*
> *bar sinister*
> *of anchovies*

Cwm Marchnant

I wave to the valley's "last good man"
standing in the yard of his farm, bright
with new red paint. Further up there is only
bog, rank grass, and ruins.

> *Restlessness*
> *of shorn sheep*
> *the tall thistles*

In an ash grove lies a small ruin partly
rebuilt -- a skilful job. Then something went
wrong and one morning they just upped

and left. Still pegged on the line is a little pair of trousers faded by years of rain and sun. And in the grass lies the carcass of a piano. Nearby –

> *Trashed trailer*
> *address book*
> *without addresses*

Also inside is a tidy pile of unwashed dishes, three unused tins of head lice ointment ("Enough for All the Family"), some Mozart tapes, and *The Tale of the Three Little Pigs* open in the toy box.
In warm rain I head on further up the valley, towards the rectangular greenery of a conifer plantation.

> *Beyond the taut wire fence*
> *ruined home*
> *loud with stonechats*

It was a big farm, of fine masonry. Now grass grows through the fallen window frames. In the brick bread oven is a tiny empty nest reinforced with blue bailer twine. And round the back there's a twin seat privy.

> *Leaning ty bach*
> *livid nettles*
> *thrusting through the seat*

Crossing their clapper bridge I climb the valley head, squelching across the gathering grounds of the Marchnant -- the Horse Brook.

> *Buzzards mew*
> *the midges bite*
> *mist touches the hill*

Ahead lies the Great Wet Desert of Wales -- miles of trackless hill and bog. In gothic type the Ordnance Survey celebrates the tumbled hilltop cairns.

> *Above the prehistoric dead*
> *fluttering larks*
> *sing their hearts out*

The Half-World

Steepening woodland path
through a five-bar gate
the summer sky

A rusty chain is wrapped round and round the gate. Beyond lie the rank pastures of the *gwartheg duon*.

In the baked earth
wandering everywhere
tracks of black beasts

Crusted cow pats lie among the quartz stones which flash white in the bracken. Here an ox tail disappears behind a clump of trees; there on the skyline a fine pair of horns appears and is gone. Now there are hoofbeats; then a distant bellow. The only beast ever to show himself face to face does not belong here:

Creamy bull
standing four square
in thistledown

Above the pastures a wood straggles on up
the hill, with a small quarry beyond.
Hacked out of the hillside, this rocky
hollow shelters a fine old larch. For decades
it has twisted and struggled up through the
slate and fought the westerly gales. Its
branches invite hands and feet, swaying up
high in the wind with the crows. Down
below,

> *Between the roots*
> *a cobwebbed buddha*
> *his hand in blessing*

Coils of frankincense waft and reek and
drift, and light flickers from candle lanterns.
Opposite is a meditation cushion built of
slate -- a firm seat on which to pass the time
of day and night. It is a Janus facing-both-
ways kind of seat. For, rising behind, is Y
Castell, the earth stronghold of *yr hen bobl* --
the ancient folk. Over a thousand feet high,
it's summit is just broad enough for a watch
tower.

> *Sheep skull*
> *through sightless sockets*
> *half a county*

A persistent folk memory of a massacre hangs about the place, though who slaughtered whom has long since been forgotten. At dusk, beyond the larch shrine, this is an uneasy place to be.

> *Beneath the larch*
> *hush of its needles*
> *in a searching wind*

Bill and Margot

Across our river, with its three green islets, there lies in the middle of my window the sloping field of Troed Bryn Hir. Rising behind it,

> *Steep wildwood*
> *trailing mists*
> *the reek of foxes*

Higher still, along the top of my window
frame, a fringe of trees stands fretted
delicate against the sky.

Three fine bay horses graze the field,
rumps to the western wind, their long black
flowing tails and manes. And sometimes,

> *Across the foaming river*
> *from the moonlit field*
> *pounding hooves*

Every morning a ritual is enacted.

> *Bent over*
> *their barrow of dung*
> *the old couple*

In this landscape of winter wind, struggling
against the rain soaked hillside, the two
hunched figures push the barrow back to
the field --- a bale of hay. They arrived two
years ago from the leaden flatlands of
eastern England and live in an old caravan
below the field. Even on mild days they are

muffled up against the cold. And the sun's visits to their bleak north-facing side of the cwm make no difference to their plodding routines. Separated by ford and up-river footbridge from the dozen scattered homesteads of the Upper Cwm, they are rarely seen on this side of the river.

They are the humble servants of their horses, which know neither saddle nor bridle.

Cwm yr Ogof

"The Valley of the Cave" is no more than a cleft in the steep valley side of the Rheidol. A racing stream has exposed this gash of grey rock in the greenery of oak and birch and ash. Above, the slope eases off in the rolling sheep-dotted pastures of Trisant (the Three Saints).

> *On a far-off road*
> *now and then a tiny car*
> *comes and goes*

I go to the Ogof whenever I feel my body dangling at the end of my mind. The start is a tiny chapel: "Bethel A.D. 1872" cut in slate above the door. Silent for decades, it was bought for a pittance so that its pine benches could be sold as garden furniture. The graveyard remains open to the local dead.

> *Worked to death*
> *lead miners' epitaphs*
> *picked out in lead*

Across the lane is a fine stand of European larch, some sixty or seventy years old. Slow growing and close textured, larch was used for ships' masts, and now for long-life fencing stakes. Of weaker fibre are the nearby Japanese larches I planted five years ago. An old man's choice. Some are already taller than me.

A stile leads into dense woodland which will overwhelm the path in another two or three years. Trampling baby oaks underfoot

I lash out with the billhook, knowing
already the battle is lost. Here, lower down,
Cwm yr Ogof becomes a tree-choked,
water-loud dingle.

Topping up my cairn
fishing out
another slippery stone

A tussle up through the thickets brings me
out onto the narrow gauge railway which
snakes along the side of the main valley.
Here there is Order & Purpose. I stop, stare
and listen, but nothing ever happens.

Steel rails
curve silently
a dragonfly darts by

One of the Ordnance Survey's red
pecked rights of way runs from here up the
right side of the cwm. On the ground,
however, there is only my poor waymark
stuck in a little pile of clinker.

> *Up through the tanglewood*
> *pointing the way*
> *twig through a toffee paper*

So it's hands and knees and heather roots,
heart-pounding rib-cage, up past the cave --
a fox's den where a cloud of midges dances.

In a hollow high in the pasture lies a
triangular pond, fringed with reeds. Across
its surface waterboatmen stop and start. A
passing sheep dips its muzzle. Here the
rivulet has its beginnings, the *fons et origo* of
this whole creation.

Homewards it's a couple of miles along the
edge of the wood, and then over the fence
in a reckless woodland descent.

> *Slipping and sliding --*
> *stripping the smooth roots*
> *skinned white*

Back in my study there's strong tea with
bara brith, and Cwm yr Ogof through the
window.

*Above the computer screen
hanging valley
in the top right pane*

The Battle of Pilleth

*Above the death pits
of Celtic warriors
grove of cedars*

The four huge trees stand tall on the flanks of Bryn Glas -- the Green Hill. They were planted by Sir Richard Green-Price, Bart., in the eighteenth century, where the skulls and bones of a mass grave had come to light.

  The slope is still as steep as it was on the Feast of Saint Alban, 22nd June 1402 when Owain Glyndwr won his second victory in the war of independence. In plate armour and chain mail it must have been a sweaty, exhausting uphill flog for Earl Mortimer's men at arms. It is still heavy going, head bowed, with a twin lens reflex camera.

> *Green hill*
> *site of the battle*
> *a few daisies*

Led by Rhys ap Gethin waves of Welsh
spearmen sweep down the hill. "Sir Robert
Whitney and Sir Kinard de la Bere are
slain", laments the chronicler. Few of the
English host escape across the river Lugg,
shining and winding on the valley floor
below. At the foot of the hill is the tiny
neglected Church of Our Lady, with its
rough stone tower and low roofed nave in
stained whitewash. Behind, worn steps
lead down to a healing well, shored up
with timbers. In front, a second mass grave
lies beneath the churchyard brambles. Until
recently rusty armour, holed and dented,
hung in the church.

> *Five hundred year old yew*
> *its cool green leaves*

On the top of Bryn Glas, beneath the
golden banner of Uthr Pendragon Glyndwr
commands the battle, astride his great war

horse Llwyd y Bacsiau (Grey Fetlocks).
Today it is a quiet sunny place, with this
year's lambs gambolling about. The tinkling
little stream that rises nearby has now run
clear of blood for 597 summers.

Old battlefield
wheeling shadows
of ravens

The Grey Stone

Father Time on the weathervane
WSW
scything over green fields

Y Maen Llwyd -- The Grey Standing Stone.
Gives its name to a small farmhouse folded
into the Radnorshire hills. Around a
muddy yard are sheep pens and a barn,
now a meditation hall surmounted by a
weathervane. All silent and empty for my
seven day solitary in the lean-to.
KLONDYKE is embossed in cast iron on
the stove.

Lightness of spruce
little dried blocks
iron belly

There is room enough for shrine, cushion,
camp bed, desk, and easy chair.
The other occupant is a winter fly, who
sleeps upside down above the stove.
Each morning, two hours before dawn, she
and I and the pot belly all come to life
together

The wind whistles
the stove grumbles back
between them
I sit

Out for a pee under a starlit sky. One face of
the cheesy moon is already lit up by the sun
rising, I suppose, somewhere over England.
Owls return to their roosts in the dingle.
Back on my cushion, vast space.

Later, I sit at the little desk...

> *Morning star*
> *hiss of the pressure lamp*
> *the sutras black on white*

Turning off the lamp, staring out of the window.

> *Restless buzzing --*
> *dawn filters slowly*
> *through ragged clouds*

The bliss of morning coffee is not mentioned in the sutras. Nor marmalade on toast. I brush my teeth, and get into Dogen's *Life and Death*.

Along the track another of my kind greets me. "Nice day, it is!" The care-worn face of a farmer, heaving a dead ewe into the trailer. Later, in fading light, I wander up onto the hill. Shoulders hunched, searching as usual for something too shy to show itself. Hands tighten on the rust of an iron gate.

> *Warmed by the setting sun*
> *my skinny shadow*
> *stretching across a field*

Down in the valley the searchlight of an
occasional car, swinging round a
bend. And then ... against the evening sky,
there it is.

> *Again that thorn tree*
> *rooted to the spot*
> *standing and staring*

Again the old fool is reminded. Doffs his
cap, and bows to the tree. For only when
the self retires do the ten thousand things
advance and enlighten.

The Maen Llwyd is an electricity free
zone, apart from my torch. It picks out this
and that as a flood of light can never do.
Once, a fly..

Down on paper –
drawn to the torchlight heart
transparent speckled wings

And later a hatchet…

Old axe
the sway
in its haft

Here are two centuries of heat and light.
There is the generous soft light
of the Victorian lamp, the ultimate in
paraffin technology and elegance. And
the battered VALOR heater, recalling the
draughty bed sits of my youth.
The oldest exhibit stands with a box of Co-
op matches beside my bed.

Made for thick fingers
pewter candleholder
its brass snuffer

Down in the valley lies Pant-y-Dwr -- the

Watery Hollow of some ninety souls, with
the lowest temperatures in Wales, and its
most central pub, the Mid Wales Inn. A
ghostly moon, veiled in mist, floats above
the nine sodium lights.

I throw more logs into the stove, pump
up the flaring Tilley lamp, and heat a can of
baked beans.

Closing curtains
opening curtains
this long life
of nights and days

Later, I light a single candle before the pale
green figure of Kwan Yin, goddess of
compassion, austere and erect. A slender
stick of pine incense perfumes the air. Three
times the sounding bowl ripples the silence,
and the first watch of the night begins. An
hour passes, and I stretch my legs across
the passage in the cold shadows of the
meditation hall. On the other side of the
yard the weather-beaten planks of the old

barn are silver bright.

> *Slow pacing meditation*
> *reassuringly*
> *a floor board creaks*

Returning, I wrap my black robe about me
and ease my body into the last sit
of the day. The short chant has a depth and
richness that takes me unaware. Kuan Yin
stares back, with that elusive smile of hers.

> *In the murmuring stove*
> *soft cry of owls*
> *incense*
> *burnt out*

Communion

> *Ringed by tilted pagan stones*
> *the huddled church*

Four thousand years have led to this
frosty Christmas morning. Here was both a
pagan place and a pilgrim stopover on the

way to the great abbey of Strata Florida.
They crossed a two-plank bridge over a
gorge, and then came down this same track.
On the gate in wrought iron are the scallop
shells of pilgrimage.

> *Scoured rock*
> *worn hips and knees*
> *the steepening path*

Cypress, yew and monkey puzzle crowd
the churchyard amidst a confusion of
headstones. On 17th February 1856 four
babies were born to Margaret Hughes. By
the end of the month all had died. On 1st
March her five year old son passed away,
and on the 6th her 32 year old husband,
Isaac. Then, four days later this epidemic
carried off her daughter Hannah. The
headstones of her family are Margaret's
only memorial.

> *Bone hard chill*
> *long dead griefs*
> *chiselled in the stones*

I slide into a pew behind a cowled lady. Let into her black cloak is a neat bible pocket. Dafydd ap Gwilym and Samuel Pepys, with their box pew flirtations, keep me company.

> *Bare breasted ladies*
> *holding up the font –*
> *"A generous donor"*

Looks Flemish, and wildly out of place here. But, understandably, the priest at the time found it "hard to refuse". I am moved to puzzle over the Commandments, picked out in gold on a black oaken board. New words for my Welsh vocabulary.

Mildew and paraffin hang in the damp air, forming haloes round the oil lamps. None of your High Church incense here. The front pew fills with elderly ladies bundled up against the cold, completing our congregation of a dozen souls. The wheezing harmonium cranks up, but with surprising verve.

Welsh hymnal
my tongue round vowels and consonants
the hwyl *takes off*

Wele'n sefyll rhwng y myrtwydd. The solemn
rolling anthems of Williams Pantycelyn; the
mystical visions of Ann Griffiths:

> *Guide me O Thou great Jehovah*
> *Pilgrim through this barren land*

We raise the roof, and the strains of *Cwm
Rhondda* drift out over the crags and
pastures of Bryn Glas as they have these
last three hundred years. Bread of Heaven.

> *Our priest mounts the pulpit.*
> *Mary*
> *neat in her cassock*
> *her blond hair*

The sermon is about the evils of ageism.
We all nod. Mary has liberal views. Holy
Communion is on offer even for this Zen
fox.

> *The wine and the wafer*
> *on her pale finger*
> *a wedding ring*

Dafydd ap Gwilym (fl. 1320-70):
greatest of medieval Welsh poets.

Hwyl : inner power.

Stones and Shadows

> *Incised stone*
> *husband and wife each side*
> *archaic smiles*

We pose, tall and pale in our black winter coats. Only ten years old, the photo has a remote Edwardian look about it. I had propped the camera on the broken shaft of a Celtic cross. No flash. Only the February light through small round-headed windows high in the wall. After the delayed shutter release, the long exposure.

This is the oldest part of St Seiriol's church, narrow and high-roofed. It is almost bare except for the stones carved with interlacing patterns. After one and a half millennia they were brought in out of the rain

> *Shadowed gleam*
> *hard black stone*
> *coiling and twisting*

Against one wall a cabinet displays a faded red pennant: "S.S. SEIRIOL". I recall now her yellow smoke-stacks and the bright striped awnings and deck chairs, and the band playing as we steamed across Liverpool Bay. I was nine years old. 1939. That last glorious summer, all over Europe. She was dive bombed and gutted at Dunkirk.

Every ten years or so, chance brings me back here. The windswept headland of my ancestral county. I gaze across the eight hundred yards of boiling water to Ynys Seiriol, or Puffin Island.

> *Warning buoy*
> *leaning tall and rusty*
> *into the tidal race*

With each lift of the swell its bell clangs out hollowly. Pity the puffins, pickled in vinegar and spice and shipped to London, each in its own little barrel. Much earlier the hermit Seiriol had raised his beehive cell among the limestone outcrops. His austere solitude made him famous. Only stones and legends remain. Seiriol the Pale, they called him. Once a week he and Saint Cybi the Dark would walk across Anglesey and meet in the middle at the wells of Clorach. Walking west in the morning and east in the evening Seiriol's face was always shadowed.

I sit under the stone vault of the pilgrims' holy well. Left in an alcove and catching the sun --

> *Tin night candle*
> *burnt out and empty*
> *featherlight*

And down there, silver in the bubbling spring! Is that a 5p piece. A 3d "joey"? Or

just the play of light?
Today is another February, but a blue sky'd
one.

Back to the car
trailing my lengthening shadow
across cream-coloured stone

Troed Rhiw Sebon -- "The Foot of the Slippery Slope"

Bonfire of worn-out furniture
spent diesel oil's
blue cloud

The combustible past. For over four
centuries it was a tidy farm. The bachelor
brothers stare out of a faded photograph.
The stocky one in the leather jerkin is Jac.
Cymeriad he was, a character. The tall one
in the middle is Mog, in old age a wraith
standing there in the doorway. Byron,
preserved in wood smoke and whisky, was
the last to go. He was the only one I knew,
except that his English was not much more

than my *tipyn bach*. Gradually the farm
shrank: rusty corrugated iron, brambles
and half-starved dogs.

> *Old Byron dead*
> *in the scullery*
> *his one cold tap*

AD 2000. In the stable, our Volkswagen
Estate; in the scullery, our "Elite" shower.

> *Click! Click!*
> *mouse in the inglenook*
> *woodsmoke.com*

Behind stands a nineteenth century stone
barn, empty except for a veneered side-
board.

> *Roof stripped of slates*
> *through rotten slats*
> *the clouds drift by*

Covered with sheep dung is a slate
threshing floor, on which I shall spread
rugs from Turkistan. A massive cast iron

drive shaft dominates my future study.

> *Great rusty spike*
> *its head*
> *hammered flat*

Through the barn door sunlight falls on a spade. Dug into the earth long ago, still it waits.
Sitting on a seized-up reaper, I ask myself: *How can I live so different a future amidst such an enduring past?*

> *Perched on a branch*
> *my hat*
> *nods gravely back*

Perhaps the secret lies in the Long Triangle, beyond the barn, where the bridleway rises on the right to meet the stream coming down on the left.

> *Grey wads of leaves --*
> *so many autumns*
> *choke the stream*

It's a waste bit of land, too, with its crop of rough black stones and shards of scrap iron, and its brambles that trip and tear. Yet here, in my few remaining years, I shall make a Zen garden. The goddess of compassion is already present.

> *Sawn off stump*
> *mounted on a six inch nail*
> *Kuan Yin*
> *in fine bone china*

When worn out by the labour of past and future I shall sit on the tree stump opposite her. Here our neighbour Dai's sheep come down to drink. And behind rises the quiet hill of Coed Simdhe Llwyd (Grey Chimney Wood), with its mossy stones and ancient oaks.

> *Foot of the Slippery Slope*
> *same soft rain*
> *same keen wind*
> *the dead and I*

> *Yma o hyd...*
> Still here...